Dare I Express It

Poetry Series

Heal the past,
live the present,
dream the future

Volume I

Dare I Express It
– Heal The Past, Live The Present, Dream The Future | Volume 1
Copyright © 2015 Leandrea Rivers. All rights reserved.

All rights reserved. No part of this publication may be reproduced, stored in a retrieval system, or transmitted in any way by any means – electronic, mechanical, photocopy, recording, or otherwise – without the prior permissions of the copyright holder, except by reviewer who may quote brief passages in a review to be printed in magazine newspaper or by radio / TV announcement, as provided by USA copyright law. The author and the publisher will not be held responsible for any errors within the manuscript. All characters appearing in this work are fictitious. Any resemblance to real persons, living or dead, is purely coincidental.

Author and Publisher: Leandrea Rivers
www.LeandreaRivers.com
Facebook: Author Leandrea Rivers

Co Author: Dwayne McLendon | Dwayne.McLendon@yahoo.com

ISBN: 978-0-9964713-0-5

First Edition 2015

Category: Motivational / Inspirational / Empowerment / Poetry

Library of Congress Cataloging-in-Publication Data

Editor: Emily Rogers | First Source Consulting, LLC

Photographer: Yania White | www.InfinityOneMedia.com

Cover Designer: Wallace King | www.MadHouseDesignInc.com

Formatting Designer: Eli Blyden | www.CrunchTimeGraphics.com

Printed in the United States of America

Preface

"**Dare**"—How many times have you heard that word or actually in fact been *dared*? Yes, haven't we all. Well, in this phenomenal collaboration you will be just that... Dared! As you are raptured into each poem, you will find yourself reminiscing into what was (finding answers to questions unanswered), discovering purpose (why you were created, why you are where you are and where true happiness abounds). Revelations you considered forever lost will now become plausible. Each poem will embrace you...

The element of surprise is immediately experienced after you open the pages—be prepared. Each poem is relatable. You will recognize the paths traveled in your *own* life and countless others' lives. The brilliance of this collaboration is... Guess what? There is an explanation! Each poet unveils the mask that so many never are privy to see—where the ink and pad capture the thoughts, the emotions and the fears that created each unique poem... your invitation to explore the poets' worlds...

Two perspectives of life, but all relatable encounters originating from unique spaces in time... what more can one ask? ***Dare I Express It*** is a series of collaborative poems you will happily come back to read time and time again. There is peace in each still moment in these writings that will leave you *breathless, defined* and equip you with a *relentless* zeal to conquer living life.

Dare I Express It*...*

HEAL THE PAST,
LIVE THE PRESENT,
DREAM THE FUTURE

Table of Contents

Preface iii

Life Is About Seasons
By Leandrea Rivers

Introduction – Life Is About Seasons 3
I've Loved Them All 4
I Should Have Been 6
I Don't Want To Be That Person 8
I Wish I Hadn't Told You 10
Your Worth Sign 14
Respect Me 16
Anything 18
Words Spoken 22
My Motivating You 24
Except You 28
I'm Just Saying 30
As We Collide 34
My Refuge 36
This New Me 38

Judgements
By Dwayne McLendon

Introduction – Judgements 43
Don't Judge Me 44
He Who Controls Time 46
Life's Detours 48

No Assembly Required	50
I'm For Real	52
Fine Wine	54
Who Says Men Don't Cry?	56
Ill-Fated	58
Love Vs. Lust	60
Friendships	62
Friend Or Foe?	64
Ego	66
Life's Journey	68
Acknowledgments	71

Life
Is About Seasons

By Leandrea Rivers

Dare I Express It

Introduction – Life Is About Seasons

Life...what is *life* really? ... Why am I here? What is my purpose? What am I doing with my *life?* *D*o I have power over my *life? A*ll of these questions arise in our thoughts at some point. *Life* is about seasons**...**funny how the seasons of life parallel actual weather seasons, wouldn't you agree? Many of us have endured brutal *winters*, rainy *springs*, thunderous *summer rains* and the newness of the fresh air of *fall. Each of these seasons repeat themselves,* over, and over, and over again! Year after year after year, it becomes more and more cumbersome repeating these cycles...is this because we *are not* growing or learning from our interactions with others? If our lives have been divinely purposed and God has allowed our paths to cross, why do we continuously endure such harsh seasons of life?

    I invite you to share my seasons of life - seasons of immense joy, deep pain, misperceptions and, heartfelt reflections. In this collection of poems, you will witness educational moments life unknowingly teaches...in fact, many of us have had an "award winning" season when we should have won a Grammy – a true winner! The key to unlocking continuously harsh seasons is the ability to *go through* and *make* it. Who can sing your life's song better than you? Only you!

    Life is a beautiful gift. Let's learn how to make **every day** worth living. I welcome you into my seasons of life. Inhale this poetic experience and at it's end, I guarantee you will exhale *a* positively **new** season!

I've Loved Them All

Smiling because I've loved them all–
As a woman learning to handle conflict with peace and resolve
No shade thrown,
It's true, our relationship has helped me to evolve

I'm thankful for the friendships I've encountered along the way
Hate them? No!
That would be foolish, "Wouldn't you say?"

Following your dreams can sometimes leave others amiss,
Not everyone in your camp will be overjoyed with bliss.
Where I am today,
Has taken *sacrifice*, *dedication* and *commitment* in many ways
We all have a path which *will* lead us someday.
Don't hold yourself responsible if one goes astray–
For your life you took responsibility and chose the route to sunnier days

In the end,
It was never *just* about me–
Dear Lord, open their eyes, please allow them to see …
I loved them all

"**H**e/she is truly a genuine, loving and kind-hearted person." How many times have we overheard this description of others' characters? Most of us, right? Your *actions*, not solely your *words* I believe, truly define your character. *"I loved them all"* is a defense of *character; a* response to negativity that was overheard, read *or,* a response to confrontation by someone who once acted as a team player—or so we thought. How we choose to respond to unfavorable energy can have an everlasting and profound effect on us. As we mature, we should learn how to recognize and handle differences of opinions. We should acknowledge change and handle situations in an adult fashion that is conducive to reaching a resolution. Unfortunately, not always will we find a happy medium. Does this mean we cannot demonstrate positive communication skills—especially when others are paying such close attention to us; scrutinizing our walks as Christians, parents, and our overall relationships with others?

Let's face it… God shifts us when He is good and ready–sometimes, we aren't always willing participants. We at times, put up a fight, kicking and screaming along the way. No matter how we are led to our God given purpose in life, we *will not* please everyone…. We cannot expect everyone to wish us well nor should we beat ourselves up about them not cheering us along. Everyone serves a purpose in our lives; maybe, just maybe their purpose has been fulfilled. You are living and pursuing *your* dreams–perhaps, it just isn't their season. Either way, you have no time to worry about the negativity occurring around you…stay focused, know that your *love* for them is and will always be genuine. Know that you've *loved them all* and will continue to–let's keep it moving! We must pray that they will tap into their own personal storehouses of joy, happiness, purpose and prosperity so that by the end of their journey, they too would have loved them all.

I Should Have Been

While you were searching for a love–
I should have been
All the many things you felt within
You wanted a union, where our souls could blend
Well, you had it all along, in me
It's me–
I should have been

Oh darling, the days go by—
Did you ever for once consider giving *us* a try?
I still desire …
Wanting you always by my side
Why are you still searching …
When I should have been your wife, lover and friend?
It's me
I should have been

I Should Have Been

It's simple–most have been here. We had that *one love* we thought that should have been and we somehow missed the opportunity due to circumstances, chance or pure luck. Yet, in the back of our minds, we sometimes reminisce about the love we felt. "I should have been" with that special someone–sometimes that longing will never, ever go away no matter how hard we resist; we continually convince ourselves that "***I should have been***."

I Don't Want To Be That Person

I don't want to be that person who causes you harm
Or do anything which triggers an alarm,
I'd like to be the one who is *real* without rehearsing–
Doing all there is by being a genuine person

I don't want to be that person who is amused by belittling others
That's what *mean girls* do, hate on one another
I want to be that role model you can aspire to,
Someone you'll know and trust will remain true
Please do me a favor–
Never doubt these words I'm saying to you!

I want you to have faith that I'll travel the seven seas for you …
Assisting in your courage to make all of your dreams come true–
Alive, revived and forever anew

I don't want to be that person who will make you cry
Never in my heart would I care to ever say goodbye
I want to be the person whose words are in tact
Someone whose worth is more valuable–
Simply put,
A class act!!!

I don't want to be that person

I Don't Want To Be That Person

Most of us in our hearts sincerely want to become 'a better person' but some of us don't know how.... Where to start, where do we begin? First, we have to understand that it won't be by our strength alone! You will truly have to ask God to *renew* you; renew your mind, heart and spirit–every fiber and being of your existence. A *cleansing* must take place "create in me a clean heart …" Have an honest conversation with God and confess that you know that you cannot do it without Him. It is also important that you have an 'accountability partner'–someone you can trust, one who you truly believe has your best interest at heart.

Let's be transparent–we already know the areas where we struggle the most; whether it's profanity, reckless behavior, unforgiveness, gossiping, or just being a downright *ugly* and unloving person on the inside. Yes, some struggles will be far more difficult than others, but you must not faint–keep working hard at it, keep pushing towards the mark! After all is said and done, you'll realize what you've been doing wasn't so fun after all; the hurt, shame to yourself and especially to others. The beauty of desiring to become a better person is "the reward." It comes and others will see it! You'll know once you've heard those words, "Wow, you have certainly changed–if *you* can change, *I* most certainly can." It is a beautiful thing having both the *will* to change and possessing self-control. Look in the mirror, is the person described as unforgiving, full of strife, bitter and rage staring back at you? **I don't want to be that person**, do you?

I Wish I Hadn't Told You

It's safe for me inside these walls
Only taking peeks, letting the light crawl
Friends, family, and foes wondering what has me so secluded behind storm doors
Was it something that someone said?
Something that someone did?
What could be going on inside this pretty woman's head?

Live, breathe, gather yourself and become FREE
But what is really *free* for me
Others can never embrace my personality–
Without retaining some form of jealousy

Hate me, *envy* me …
Why? Because I have Jesus' type of love rooted deeply inside of me?
Perfect? Definitely, I am not
Forgiveness *others* easily don't hand out

Again, it is safe for me inside these walls
Throughout these corridors I walk and can stand tall
Outside, the world chops at me, attempts to make me feel small
Will there ever be someone out there who will accept me flawed?
The world points and expects me to see,
Why won't they just let *me* be *Me*?
Is it too much to ask—
To accept my love unconditionally?

Inside these walls, I cannot remain locked
For outdoors is where my happiness will forever be sought

I Wish I Hadn't Told You

To see butterflies so beautiful flying free—
To feel the sand between my toes
And the earth beneath my feet...
These are the places where my heart will forever be caught
One day Lord, these walls will come down
For a good fight I would have fought

Wish, I hadn't told you!!

* * *

A time comes when you've learned to accept the trials you've endured and you are no longer concerned with others' opinions of *your* life choices, but that wasn't always the case. Perhaps there was a time when all that ever mattered was the opinion of others–you attempting to please the entire world and what they thought really mattered most to you .... Thank God for growth–understanding that you are not perfect; yet, your imperfections have matured you into the sound person you are today.

We sometimes confide in the wrong people; those we feel who love us and only want happiness for us, but in reality, not everyone in our playing field is there to cheer us out of the storm. Some people are there to see us get trampled and watch us fumble or lose. Thank God for God Almighty–He will give you a place of escape, but that won't come before you've had to shield yourself and find a safe place of refuge—to seek His deliverance, His guidance and His purpose for your life.

Once you've been elevated to higher heights, you can become free from those who cornered you behind those storm doors–too afraid to come out ...unaware of who to trust. Many of us have had countless disappointments; betrayals of friends, loved ones or failed romantic encounters–we *wish we hadn't told them* how we truly felt. We opened ourselves up and became vulnerable realizing that we shared personal information, fears and hurts we would have been better off sharing only with God Himself. We must be careful to choose our circle of friends with wisdom and discernment. Know that secluding yourself only denies you of all of the promises God has stored up for you. I wish I hadn't told you because I wasn't sure if you were someone who was for me and wanted me to win in life. Now in hindsight, I realize God will always be *for me* and with Him, I will never fail! Either way I choose I will win!

Dare I Express It

Your Worth Sign

Your worth is more than they assign
Your closed door needs to have a *Do Not Disturb* sign
Or better yet, the *Do Not Deserve* kind
Or you'll get *Kicked To The Curb* if you don't *Heed My Word* sign
Read Between The Lines for surely I cannot believe you've *Lost Your Mind* sign...

I pulled you aside
In an attempt to get you realigned
Hoping you would clearly read all of the *fine* print lines

A new love,
I hope your heart will bleed
For my heart–
You drained the very blood out of me,
Causing me to have triple bypass heart surgery!

Your excuses no more
It's time you step towards the *exit* written above the door—
I'm walking head held high,
Looking up towards the clear blue sky
For in it exudes eternal love for me
I wish you a life full of happiness and glee

The signs are *now* posted:
Do not Disturb, Do Not Deserve, Kicked To The Curb, Heed My Word, Read Between The Lines and *Lost Your Mind* signs ...
To proceed any further—
Karma will surely 'pencil you in' to your *Appointed Day In Time* sign!

We are *all* valuable and should equally understand our self-worth; no one should feel as though they are superior to another. *Respect* comes to mind when I think about one's "worth sign." It is simple–who has time to be disrespected whether they be male or female? It all boils down to respect!

A person who has no respect for you will lie, cheat, steal and only God knows what else. Don't be afraid to show the exit door to those who make you form *signs*–it doesn't mean they can't come back through! You are giving them an opportunity to exercise growth and to understand you will no longer tolerate messy behavior or negative tendencies in *your* realm of *peace* and *tranquility*.

It isn't always a romantic interest or a mate who hurts you–it could be a parent, sibling, friend or co-worker, anyone who claims to have a *love* for us! Unfortunately, there are certain type of *loves* we probably shouldn't have in our lives and if that means loving them at a distance–so be it. Please just remember, holding on to resentment and bitterness will only hurt *you*. Therefore, if you give them a *sign*–do it with *all* intention of being able to forgive as well. How valuable is **your worth sign**?

Respect Me

It's easy...
All I ask is that you respect me
Neither will lose if we handle our differences with calm and ease
No need to build each other up,
Only to tear back down—
Far too many do this when others aren't around

To respect me—
Is more rewarding,
Agree or disagree
Life is *real* it isn't a toy—
To play it as a game may cause your very life to be destroyed

All I've ever asked from the beginning is again "that you respect me"

Respect Me

Let's face it, many of us are on our *second* or *third* marriage by now and unfortunately, there are still far too many who simply don't understand the basic concept of good old-fashioned R-E-S-P-E-C-T (in my *soulful voice*).

There are many who "did their dirt" and even in their sins, they did everything possible to avoid being found out or caught in the act. *Nowadays*, no one has respect for themselves or for others; it is solely about self-gratification; they could care less if others see their sins–they are instead, somehow *glorified*.

If you lived in a glass house and all the world could see how you lived behind the doors–would you behave any differently? Of course you would–so let us no longer *act* as though "the world is not watching." Let's live *right* because we understand that Christ *is* watching.

If we demonstrated respect for those we love and because our *character* calls for us to respect those we do not necessarily as they say, "get along with" maybe, just maybe, we could make a change in the *hearts* of those who watch our actions; our *children*, *family*, *friends* and perhaps *co-workers* ....

Oh, trust me...everyone is taking notes on your life; at the end of the day, will this cause you to "**respect me**?"

Anything

Another day,
And here I am open to the possibilities of *anything*

No, yesterday I could not believe that today would bring a brighter day …
Yet, here I am with joy–
Unspeakable joy …
Tomorrow, more possibilities *anything*

Years, come and years go …
Reminiscing the old times, longing for more good times and wondering, *What is left in this present lifetime?*
Hmmm …you remind yourself "just about *anything*"

Today, I know I can be "anything" I want to be, it is our Lord and Savior Jesus Christ who strengthens me, "anything" is possible, if you believe; Jesus says, "Have faith in ME!"

Hope gives you strength
It gives you peace when you feel like you can't go on–
Anything you desire you can acquire if you have enough hope to continue the race

Issues, we all have them—*anything* can become an issue–
It's up to you how you will resolve
God can handle *anything* He's your best friend …
A gentle ear to listen whenever you call, so why do we time and time again ignore Him as if He doesn't exist at all?

Not I, I would have said if you told me that I would be where I am today …

Anything

Looking back, I realize *anything* can happen in this cycle called "life" presented as a gift each day

God, wants us to appreciate the things of this life, but most importantly to love and obey Him who sacrificed so that we may live our lives …that through Him, we may have "***ANYTHING***"

* * *

Many take for granted how very blessed they are–there was a time I did. Life can happen in ways we never imagined and sometimes it *shakes* us up a bit. It's true, *anything* can happen in this *life,* presented as a gift each day …what will you do with it? *Anything*?

We have so much power to control most of what happens in our lives–it begins in our *minds*. Positive thoughts, positive actions, positive habits …overall *positivity*. Sometimes, *joy* truly does come in the morning and for others it may take a bit longer. I encourage you to hang on–the world hasn't heard half of my stories and I continue to hang on! I honestly admit to my lack of poor discernment …. Somehow it all worked out for my *good* in ways I could not ever have dreamt, even in my best dream. We must keep *hope* alive and prevalent in our hearts–*your* time is coming, hold on!

This poem *Anything* derived from a friend who called me one day–he was serving a military tour overseas; he asked for prayer and encouragement as friends do, but on this particular day he asked for something a little *different*. My friend asked that I write a poem–and the obvious question was of course, "About what?" He said, "Anything!" I repeated, "Anything?" *Me*, being the literal person that I am, had ink and pad all ready to go …I began to write …*reminiscing the old times, longing for more good times and wondering,* "What is left in this present lifetime?" Anything?

Understand friends, *anything* in this life can produce the highs and the lows–the ins and the outs and everything in between, I encourage you, do not take for granted this precious gift we continue to be granted.

What is left in this life for you? Again I ask ...***anything***?

Words Spoken

Living in a world oh so cold
People not realizing how much their words cause effects—taking tolls
Sometimes never really understanding how much so
Until they have crossed that bridge called "growing old"

The flashing lights, memories creeping up throughout the nights, circling like a dome
Once, twice, three times opening my eyes to capsized stories untold—
Reappearing at times unbeknownst to me
How, when, why, what did I do to deserve this insanity?
Deaf ears, blurred vision others can't hear nor see
Words spoken …play, rewind, somebody please erase these!

Next time around, guaranteed my words would not be spoken in haste
Don't take for granted family, friends and loved ones–instead let us rephrase
To each one, please think with wisdom, love, and humility before we speak
To venture upon another path will eventually lead to your defeat–
For entering into the Kingdom requires effort and a spirit of being meek
To speak foolishly is unwise if Christ is Whom you truly seek.

Words Spoken

Is there a *new* definition of "being a Christian?" In this new age, many are saying whatever is on their hearts and minds without any form of censorship; do you feel this is acceptable to Christ? I honestly feel there are people who have died from broken hearts–irreparable damage caused by uncensored *harsh* words. True or false? *True.* We need to be aware of the possible harm and hurt we can cause someone else. A soft word goes a long way …I think at times how different my life could possibly have been if I only learned sooner in life, to hold my tongue. Was it worth the **words spoken**?

Dare I Express It

My Motivating You

My motivating you–
Was it your demise?
Or did 'my motivating you' lead you to happier times?

I pushed you towards the mark of the things you dared to dream
Later realizing–
You never wanted spotlight, money nor the bling!
Others can sometimes bring the worst in you out ...
In my heart,
I only wanted what was best for you
Will you ever understand that was *my truce* sweetheart?

It's funny,
I never thought after all was said and done that I'd be the one to lose
Lose the friendship that never had a chance to bloom
Allowing the flesh to get us caught up in lusts of rapture
Time once again had so eloquently captured ...
Our countless mistakes as mothers and fathers
But, by those same mistakes here we are again marching
A bright, promising day ahead
Without the comforts of one another's bed
Yet, instead *finally* thinking with the right head
God has an amazing way of getting His glory,
Who would have thought in the end we'd share our stories!

My Motivating You

As seasoned adults, we never know when that opportunity will come along to have dialogue with a *love* from our past. When it does happen, prayerfully, each one has experienced growth and can honestly and openly express what could never have been said in the past. Why couldn't those words have been previously spoken? First, because we had no knowledge of what was happening at that time or second, we didn't know how to discuss our *true* feelings.

Our intentions for someone else to thrive in life may be completely 100% genuine, but if the other person is not in a place of acceptance or receptiveness, it is pointless–they will fight you tooth and nail. It is important to always try to see the best in others, but there are so many who don't see the best in *themselves*. The result: your efforts come forth as being pushy, bossy or just a total mismatch. We must meet people where they are–you may not be the one who will follow them where they are going and if where they are *currently* is causing *you* to be displaced emotionally, spiritually, socially (or you're overall just *settling)*, recognize that God can give you the pass to exit; be kind and do so quietly, without kicking and screaming.

Often we see someone and think, "Wow, this person has great *potential.*" One would think it is better to motivate and encourage them right? Wrong! Wrong, especially if the other person is not *mentally* and *emotionally* prepared. I'll say it a million times if I have to, "Everyone we meet isn't meant to be a mate." The sooner that is understood–the happier *some* lives will become.

"People come into our lives for a reason, a season or a lifetime" and only time determines which will apply. Recognizing the difference is the true value in being a "motivator" to someone, especially those you truly love–we must understand the role we play in each other's lives. Many are placed in our lives for a temporary purpose or for a season–plant your seeds and understand God may destine others to water them.

Ask yourself, will you motivate them to take steps and help them to bend (compromise) or will you be the one to help them *spring* forward? Perhaps you'll be the one that finally convinces them to *jump*! Either way, know when your purpose has been served. Sometimes, it takes a person God has specifically chosen to *push* them over the edge into their destiny. Accept your role, and accept where people are. It may or may not be *your* purpose to serve–*if* that is your scenario…in time, the lesson will be retained for its proper use, "God never, ever wastes a hurt."

"Timing is everything" and *most* things in life become clearer in time–God sees and knows all. He appoints a perfect time for a reunification designed to excel each party to new heights and you best believe that time won't come a minute sooner than God allows!

It is no longer about your level(s) of vulnerability–especially when physical intimacy is no longer on the table; each party can freely open up without repercussions *or* being lured by intimacy or past pleasures. Finally, discussions of truth can be waved as "white flags" of peace and understanding in this relationship, even though you were once *lovers*. **My motivating you**, was it truly your demise?

Except You

They want to put on these façades
Pretending to be ballers and "party like rock stars"
Their artificial and deceptive plans to get yet another in their beds
 ALL...Except you

They want to whisper sweet nothings in your ear–
Trying to persuade you that their words are truly *them* being sincere
 ALL...Except you

Why, they want to sneak into dreams causing nightmares in the dark hours
Brushing up against daytime minutes causing frozenness in undaunted silence
ALL...Except you

Why, must they smell so good
Look so nice
Body so tight
Get you all hooked and then take flight?
ALL...
Except you

They say they want to take care of you
Shape and mold you
Help to unfold the real you–
That no other can complete you
ALL can't, Except you

"Except you, are you saying you are *not* like the rest?"

Except You

"Except you, are you *not* afraid to give your very best?"

"Except you, why should I believe *you* and *only* you?"

"Except you, do you know how many others started off just like *YOU*???"

I am the *exception* "men/women" say,
I am the *exception* "he/she" says...
I am the *exception* "they" all say!!!

"Except you, what makes you *Exceptional*?"

* * *

For starters, you can't change *anyone*. Let's be completely 100% in agreement here! You can however, influence others–you, being in someone's life can totally enhance everything about them. You thinking you are an exception to everyone else in their past is completely delusional. Everyone has played a role by the time you've entered into this *new* person's life–therefore, you *are not* the exception ...you are the *next* friend, girlfriend, boyfriend, fiancé, wife or husband. If it be the Lord's will–let us pray that you are their *last*.

There will always be some form of residue around and if you think not, you're sadly mistaken. No one else is great *except you*? Oh, really? Please, *never* get *too* comfortable in your role–stay at your very best. Whatever you did to *get* that person, continue to do so to *keep* them! Again, the question is asked ... **Except you**, what makes you exceptional?

I'm Just Saying

What is really going on inside of your brain
Did you really do it—
Without a plan?
Man that was lame!!!
I'm just saying ...

What has happened to our culture
Our respect for our elders
The Bible!
Did you really think we would let this go
Without you being chastised and accounted for?
You, getting rich–
While stealing from our poor!

You have no respect for yourself
And expect him to?
It's not his fault
With your body
You are so loose
Girl, you better hold your head up
Get a clue!!!
You wonder why our kids are strapping nines (9mm)
Did you for once
Spend just a little time?
Calling him your son
Yet, passing by him so fast
You couldn't see that he needed you–
We love the world
More than we love our own flesh and blood
Where or where did we take that wrong turn?

I'm Just Saying

If, what I'm saying
Is cutting you deep
Stop this vicious cycle now
Don't repeat!!!
Don't get mad at the messenger
The human race needs help
Can't you see!!!

I'm just saying…

* * *

It is far time for everyone to stop placing the blame on others and accept accountability for our own personal actions. What happened to the African Proverb "It takes a whole village to raise a child?" This is a group effort folks–we cannot continue to watch our children suffer when we are capable of devoting our time, finances and wisdom to guide our youth. There was a time when we took pride in working together to enrich the lives of others; tomorrow is not promised to any of us, we must bring about change today! Our children are killing one another, they have no guidance–we spend much time on so many other things we deem important but nothing is more important than our future (our children). Women, we set the examples for our young girls to respect their bodies *and* how we will, and will not allow men to treat us. Ladies, please remember "you are what you *answer* to." A lady will always love herself first in order to have an ability to love others effectively. Any woman can be a woman, but not every woman can be a "lady"—understanding the difference will separate a lady from *any* ordinary woman.

Our families–stop with the jealousy of others' successes, instead let us help one another achieve success. There are various cultures where multiple families are living in one household or sharing one vehicle; they are all sacrificing to help one family at a time buy their first home or get a reliable vehicle. In today's economy, we need to reach deeper to help our loved ones, but understand the difference between helping and being an enabler. We need to build a legacy. What will you leave your children, grandchildren …anything?

Parents there was never a manual on parenthood; we did the best we could and of course, we made some mistakes. It is never too late to correct them! Perhaps you were unable to provide an education, spend quality time …you are still here, it's not too late! The past is the past and *now* can be the appointed time when everyone involved reaches a turning point. The life you may have wanted to provide to your children, you can now provide to your grandchildren, especially if you didn't have the tools before to guide your own children.

Every day is an opportunity to cultivate change in some capacity for the betterment of cultures, communities, countries, youth, families and our individual circumstances.

"I never lose, either I win or I learn." Understand that every experience and purpose was created to help us live in P.E.A.C.E. Can we all at least try? **I'm just saying.**

As We Collide

You don't know me
And I, you neither
Yet, you deny me three times–
Like Peter denied Jesus

Walk a mile in my shoes
Before you go judging me
Were you there each time–
Simultaneously!!!

Our paths crossed unmistakably
No doubt—
For a reason
Only time will determine
You, liking
And me, pleasing
If time shared
Was merely *a season*

As we collide
Our stories will be our guide–
To heal the past
Live the present
And dream the future

But, how will *you* know?
When your heart remains so guarded and cold—
Unwilling to allow me to explore beneath the sores

I heard your words—
I felt them deep

As We Collide

I stepped back
To my safety zone
Ready to retreat

My heart …
Thump, thump
Not skipping a beat
You, my dear–are wrong
I am very much complete!

I don't need you
To slap me with words
Attempts to make me feel weak
With or without you
Love is worth hitting repeat.

* * *

Whether we will admit or not, we all carry some type of baggage. We meet individuals in life and we prejudge or misjudge them without even taking the time to have a conversation with them. We judge based on their appearance, what others may have said or by pictures displayed on social media. We deny their attempts to have a conversation without hearing their purpose for reaching out–your encounter isn't always for your benefit (instead, it can be God using *you* to benefit *them*). We must be careful with *words* we project onto others–we don't know how deep their sores extend. There are some who are afraid of love and deny attempts to building *any* type of relationship– possibly even one that may lead to 'the love you've always dreamed of.' We must be bold to hit repeat; it doesn't always have the same outcome—that skip in the song may actually play smoothly this time around …. **As we collide** … are you ready?

My Refuge

God has blessed me,
He has given me serenity–
A place of peace;
Beauty and tranquility.

My refuge is a place where my dreams remain alive
It is a place that every time I think of …
It places a beautiful smile which spreads wide

It is a joy no words can conform
My refuge separates me from the despairs of this world
Finally, there is a place where I can return and rest safely–
My refuge,
My home!

My Refuge

Sometimes we can seek refuge in the wrong place, completely out of God's intended will for our lives. We are deceived by our own perceptions of what our desires are–ultimately, time reveals this *refuge* was merely for a season (a place to rest but for a moment).

This refuge brought us comfort for that present hour, but a lifetime of peace is only experienced when there is evidence of God's true source of love–God's type of love is never submerged in lies, secrets, nor deception.

A home must sit on a solid foundation–its walls must be secure. Anyone can set up a beautiful and exquisite house, but it can never become a home (a place of refuge) if there is no peace or unity. Ask yourself, what is **my *refuge*** built on?

This New Me

This new me
The world is now privy to see
My eyes are beholding endless possibilities of what's yet to be
I stretched myself wide and held my head high
Not always understanding the what's, when's where's and the why's
I've looked to the hills entrusting my help
For Jesus' promise He has faithfully kept
My past I recognize as a part of my growth
Looking forward and beyond is where my eyes are bestowed
The self-love I now have I've humbly packed
No man or woman can ever resort me back
Forgiving others has allowed me a clean slate
You can look them in their eyes now and honestly say, "Today indeed is a lovely day."

So often we put on façades pretending that all is great within our spirit man and lives when in actuality, we are a complete mess! This poem speaks about finding self-love and facing those people associated with your past hurts and being okay with seeing them because you truly have come to love *who* you are, *where* you are and *all* of the great things ahead. **This new me** is "Fabulous darling!" EXHALE

HEAL THE PAST,
LIVE THE PRESENT,
DREAM THE FUTURE

Dare I Express It

Introduction – Judgements

Realistically, some may say we (men) don't change, that what we portray is just who we really are …. I'm a man and like many, my life has not been "up to par." There is no need for you to be sympathetic. I made my own choices and some were down right pathetic. They say I'm a charmer, the stereotypical "ladies man." What you see and decipher is not accurate, that's not who I am now—my request; unchain your mind, stereotypical thoughts are a form of imprisonment. I invite you to explore beyond what you see and relinquish any prejudices....

Don't Judge Me

Please don't judge me because of my physical
I am humble and quiet by nature and personally, your judgements are unfounded and critical.

Don't judge me by my scowl
My facial features are intended to keep those away who can and will not understand my style.

Don't judge me because of others' opinions
Judge me after a discussion and then you can form a decision.

Don't judge me from afar
Judge me after I let you in the life of a man whose life has been marred by his own personal scars.
Never judge a book by its cover because you limit your mind and leave many pages undiscovered.

Don't Judge Me

How many times have we been judged based on hearsay, our physical appearance or negative assumptions? *"He looks so mean." "I bet he thinks he is all that."* Or, *"He is so quiet, he is probably so sneaky."* I've heard it all. LOL! I'm basically a laid-back guy who keeps to himself but because of the scowl I regularly display or my physique, I continue to be labeled with many negative assumptions. We need to have conversations with people first, and then we can form our opinion of them. Once someone opens up and they realize you can be trusted, then you will get to know the true person. Until then, **Don't Judge Me**.

He Who Controls Time

I wish I could go back and do it all over again
Every mistake—
Bad decision and Lord knows …all the sins,
I wish I could change the hands of time …
Only if I could go back with this state of mind
Wisdom and maturity would be my guide.

I persevered through obstacles that many have failed
God controlled the boat that I sailed
Now here I stand with purpose and hope
A living testimony I am and that's no joke.

He Who Controls Time

Don't we all wish we could go back in life and do it all over again? All of the countless mistakes and mishaps we encountered would hopefully be changed. Would we be the person we are today without those lessons of life? God has a purpose for our lives and that purpose has already been written. Embrace your struggles and realize they have given you growth as an individual. Where would I be if I had never struggled or had to deal with obstacles? I am thankful for setbacks in my life because they made me stronger mentally. When an obstacle or challenge comes my way now, I know that I'm battle tested and I know I can survive the storm …. After all, **He who controls time** will forever be by my side.

Life's Detours

You can say I know a little about relationships,
I've been around the block twice–
The first I was a little scarred but the second actually bettered my life
Distraught, hurt, sad I turned into positive energy...
I'm living life for me and not those enemies
Of course I made mistakes so who am I to blame?
Too often we don't look at our reflection and that's a shame
Often I am asked would I do it again?
Let's just say I'm open but only God knows when
In this newfound me I have to catch myself at times …
You can get caught up thinking with your eyes and not your mind
It's a curse that most men can't cure
So often we try to go right,
but we often end up at the detour!

Life's Detours

I have been around the block a time or two–I was married twice but due to circumstances and situations, I'm back on the battlefield. My first marriage was an ideal situation that I was truly not mature and ready to handle. Great woman, but I was still straddling the fence with women and alcohol and that destroyed my first marriage. The second time I had matured and was 'all in' but unfortunately, it takes two to build a relationship—especially when blended families are involved. But, I also had to look in the mirror and realize that I'm not perfect and I needed to work on myself. Now, I'm single again and I know the "do's and dont's" of single life. The women and attention I don't feed into because I know what I desire and there's no need to waste my time nor theirs.... The "flesh" is something else; men have sexual needs and we often get caught up in the flesh. We have to ask ourselves at those moments, is self-gratification worth these few moments .... **Life's detours**?

No Assembly Required

No assembly required,
I want to be the total package–
No assembly required
No games and ready for marriage ...
No parts to put together,
I'm preassembled and won't fold under pressure

No broken promises or false pretenses,
Only honesty and sincerity are my wishes
I am the physical and mental that your heart desires,
When we come together our love will be the kind that your girlfriends admire
A complete man I am and not a boy,
I'll nurture your heart and not treat it as if it were a toy
I'll do the little things that will make you smile
And keep you close to my soul all the while ...
I am no assembly required.

No assembly required. Ladies, how many of you want that man that comes complete, no assembly required? The total package, he has put away his toys, childish ways and he's ready to enjoy his queen. He has been through some things so he is experienced in relationships and truly knows what a woman wants and requires. He is physically and emotionally ready to face the challenges head on and deal with them as a man does and not as a boy. He is ready to love you for you and not for what you can provide or what you can do for him. He fills the voids where you may not be complete. He is what you desire, **NO ASSEMBLY REQUIRED**.

I'm For Real

Look here I'm trying to be as real with you as I can
I'm not your typical or average man
I'm currently on a journey called *doing me*
Making a better life and controlling my destiny
I've had some misfortunes in this thing called life
I'm no longer Mr. Do Wrong,
I'm trying to be Mr. Do Right.
I'm currently setting goals and living my dreams
I don't know if my heart is ready for you to be on my team
I'm being real and not trying to play with your emotions
But are you listening or waiting on a promotion?
I know that you don't like your status or position
Currently it's all I can offer in this rendition
When the time is right our destiny will be decided
Right now accept my honesty and realize you are not being misguided.

I'm For Real

Have you ever been in a situation where it is perfect but the timing is not right? Some people come into your life when you are working on "self." It's not a knock down on them but, unfortunately you are not ready or can't provide what they need in their life at the moment. You may have been through some unfortunate situations and you realize that you're not ready to give your heart freely at this time in your life. You don't want to mislead them, so you are honest and upfront but they currently desire more. We have to realize if it's God will, it will be. The question is, are you patient enough to wait on God's will? **I'm for real**.

Fine Wine

Often times we see the signs,
but we get caught up because they were just too fine
Caught up in the physical appearance because we couldn't think rationally
Thinking with our lower extremities and ignoring their personality
The lust demon has taken over our thoughts …
We're driving but everything is a blind spot
It's hard to focus when all you can see is a prize
How many of us have got caught up by only thinking with our eyes?

Fine Wine

We all know that men are attracted to the physical. The first things that catch our eye on a woman are her face and her body. If the face and body are intact, well, the rest is usually history. We tend to not think about where she is mentally or socially. All we see is "the prize" and this is where the problems arise—knowing this woman for only her physical qualities. Because we are solely focused on the one goal to have sex with this woman, we're basically lusting over her for her physical attributes and ignoring whatever baggage that comes along with her. How many times have you been caught up with your eyes because they were **fine as wine**?

Who Says Men Don't Cry?

They say men are not supposed to cry and for this I wonder, *why*?
Is it because of society's views,
Or is it that we are too manly to express our blues?
We are taught by our counterparts not to show our emotional side,
but little do some of us know, it's *this* that makes a woman vibe.
It's okay men as long as you are secure,
but if you must know, most women realize *then* that your heart is pure
If some of us could learn to stop suppressing our feelings,
I guarantee there would be more intimate healing

Who Says Men Don't Cry?

All men are supposed to be tough guys, right? We are raised as boys to suck it up and don't cry, Act "like a man." This is what society has raised and taught us—that these are requirements to being a man. If we cry, we will be labeled as "soft" and not a "real man". So when our emotions get the best of us, what do we do? Hide and cry and keep our feelings bottled up. This is a recipe for disaster. Suppressing these emotions will only lead to mental anguish. We, as men have to understand that there's nothing wrong with showing your emotional side. We are men but we also are human. Women love men that have an emotional side. Revealing it shows that we can be compassionate and caring. Men, be secure in yourself and realize it's okay to shed a tear, **Who says men don't cry?**

Ill-Fated

I was once in your shoes,
So who am I to judge your ill-fated moves?
I lied, cheated and even manipulated,
but only life will show you how you are becoming ill fated
I played with hearts and emotions,
but no one told me that this was a wicked potion
I used what I had to get what I wanted,
And now others are emulating this unfortunate tool that I started
I was a man of many faces,
Pick one and I'll name the places...
My quest is to change your thoughts and your path
It's your choice but I don't think you want to feel this wrath

Ill-Fated

How many times have you watched from afar, someone emulating your mistakes in life? I used to be someone that had no conscience or care in the world. I was living for "self" and to feed my needs. I basically didn't care who I hurt or mistreated to get what I wanted—it was all about me. Lying, manipulating, cheating, you name it and I did it. Unfortunately most of the victims were women, I was at an immature stage in my life, and I was being reckless. The saddest part about this is I believe that what you sow, you will reap. Now, I have regular conversations with young men who are following this unfortunate path. Many are worse than I was. I attempt to counsel these young men to let them know their behavior leads to a life of destruction. Karma has a funny way of putting you in the same situation you placed others in, simply **ill-fated**.

Love Vs. Lust

Lust is the desire for the physical while love requires more of the mental
Lust will not sustain the realities of life
Love will make you understand you have to sacrifice

Lust is saying I love your body
Love will have your mind and body spinning like a disc jockey
Lust only considers self
Love puts your heart on a pedestal and not a shelf

Lust says I love you
Love does not speak,
It's understood not by words but by mystique
A boy is a perfectionist of lust but a man is a professional at love

Love Vs. Lust

Lust versus love ...a very thin line that leaves many of us confused. Oftentimes, we think we are in love with someone and it's really just physical attraction. We love the thought of how they make us feel physically. Take away the physical and let's see if you truly love this person. Are you willing to make sacrifices for them or, are you involved for your own selfish reasons? Love is an action word, we can say it all day but proving it is a different story. What makes you love this person— ask yourself, *"Is it true Agape love or lustful love?"* Do you love them like you love your kids or your parents? The next time you tell someone, *"I love you"*, ponder, is it **Lust or Love**?

Friendships

Friend, a word that many of us use so loosely
Not truly knowing the origin,
Responsibilities and duties.
Surprisingly you never know how this bond may begin...
Enemies, past lovers, are now best of friends.

Loyalty and trust are usually their best traits
There aren't too many that can serve this on their plate.
Of course you are going to have some that put on a façade
But through discernment and time you will be able to decipher the mirage.

They've been there for you through the good and bad times
Stayed by your side when you thought you were losing your mind.
True friendship is like a rare gem
When you find it, appreciate and always thank them.

Friendships

Do we really know what a true friend is? Friendship is hard to decipher because people can put on a façade for months and even years. How many of your friends have been truly loyal to you over the years? How many have stuck with you during the times that you have been wrong? Have these same 'friends' told you so? Life's lessons are learned when we prove or experience the definition of the word "friend." We have to travel through some uncomfortable situations and circumstances to recognize loyalty. True friends will not lie to not hurt your feelings or make you uncomfortable. **Friendship** involves respecting those who reciprocate respect.

Friend Or Foe?

Do you despise me for my growth?
We were raised to honor our oath
We were both afforded the same chances
Is it my fault because of your circumstances?
You are my ace boon coon
At least I thought, but now I must assume
We were at one point like Fred and Barney
Now it seems you're in the Navy and me in the Army
I would never have guessed that it would come to this
My confidant is now a part of my most hated list
Jealousy and envy are now your closet friends
Man I pray that you can detox your mind, find an effective cleanse
This really hurts me deep inside—
To realize that my friend is really Dr. Jekyll and Mr. Hyde.

Friend Or Foe?

How many of you have had a friend who you thought was your close friend, only to realize they were a foe? I mean, you trusted this person with the world and there was nothing you wouldn't do for them. Then you notice the signs; the unsupportive comments when you accomplish something good, the negativity, when they should have been celebrating. They become upset because you are accomplishing something that they can't. A friendship that was as close to true brotherhood or sisterhood now, all down the drain because of jealousy, hate and envy, It's truly a sad situation, when you loved this person unconditionally. Ask yourself again, is this person a **friend or foe**? The realization is ...your friend *is* your foe.

Ego

Secretly we compete but what is the competition?
Is it based on ego or is it unknown friction?
I'm doing me and you are doing you …
So if this is true,
What's the purpose?
I honestly have no clue!
Can we just be happy for each other's success?
It's nothing to gain and that I can attest.
If I win,
You win is our philosophy.
It appears I'm playing checkers and you're playing monopoly
Believe me when I say it's nothing to gain from this strategy—
The conclusion only leads to drama and agony.

Ego

Unfortunately, there are people that tend to base their lives on another's success. Have you ever noticed that a friend, sibling, associate or co-worker attempts to do everything you do *and* try to do it better than you? We should be happy for others' successes, but hate, jealousy and envy tend to knock at the door when we observe or hear about someone who is doing better than us. Don't allow your ego to open and step through that door! The only competition should be with the man or woman in the mirror. When you are happy with yourself, you choose *not* to engage in personal competitions …be the best *you* that *you* can be, don't be deceived by your **ego**.

Life's Journey

My plate is full and I have no more to offer
Kids, career, health and now an author
Not trying to be funny but I don't have time for some extras
I'm consumed with growth and opportunity, not fiestas.

Distractions, drama, envy and hate all knocking at my door
Attempting to steal my dreams, my future and create a mind war.

Now I've come too far to regress into this path
The tool of discernment taught me how this would contrast.

My focus and vision must stay guided towards the light
Because if I enter into this negativity,
Then I would have lost my sight.

I must not let the naysayers knock me off my quest
 Because the man in the mirror will have failed God's test.

Oftentimes as you begin a journey in life you will be tested
But at the end of the day it solely falls on YOU to follow your dreams and paths.

Life's Journey

In this poem, I am stating that I don't have time to feed distractions. I'm consumed with positive energy and I focus on engaging with only positive people. Women continuously approach me by the boat load and men say, "Who does he think he is?" Women see an opportunity in me because I'm gaining status per se, but luckily I've heard it all before and have decided I've come too far to regress. Men are watchful and emulating; that's great because I have inspired some to look within themselves and use their God given talents. I have a career that involves long and sometimes strenuous days, two energetic kids and I'm now an author. I don't have time to feed my distractions …my plate is full. This is **life's journey**.

Dare I Express It

HEAL THE PAST,
LIVE THE PRESENT,
DREAM THE FUTURE

Acknowledgments

My Everything–My God, how can I imagine making it without You, The Almighty? Your dreams are far larger than *any* we have for ourselves. I'm grateful, humbled and most importantly, *thankful* to You for keeping me through my 'seasons of life' and the many encounters along the way. You purposed this season, these *very* moments to use my gifts and talents for Your glory. Thank You.

My Family–My parents who are forever, my biggest supporters. Always ensuring my happiness at the forefront; I could not ask for better. My siblings—who love me as brothers should; there's never enough *I love you's* and *kisses* to go around. "I love you guys!" My motivators—always cheering me along: my grandmothers, aunts, uncles, cousins, close friends and especially "T Owens"; you make the statement *"People come into your life for a reason..."* an understatement! Words cannot express…. Everyone needs a shield—my prayer warriors, always there, always keeping me uplifted: T. McGriff, C. Marion, B. Armstrong, G. James-King, and countless others. I know your prayers reach God! And last, but not least…*my Heartbeat*–my son; times when I couldn't see my way…you made the vision become very clear through my love for you! I couldn't ask for more perfect gifts: my grandson–*my Prince* and our soon arrival, my granddaughter–*my Princess*. Being a "GiGi" (grandmother) is a love I never knew existed. Thank you too, the mother of my grandchildren; it would not be possible without you *sweetheart*. I am forever grateful–you have brought an abundance of true *joy* to our family.

My team of professionals–it is always a pleasure working with individuals as passionate about your craft as you are and believing in you as professionals goes even further. Thank you **Emily Rogers** (Editor), for editing my first book "The Most Loved"; we did it again—you are always on point dear! Yet again, **Eli Byden** (Book Designer), for "The Most Loved" layout and cover– here again to deliver what you do best; another beautiful *interior* layout that eloquently reflects my personality. **Wallace King** (Graphic Designer), for a *new* experience; I was nervous about bringing a new face to the team, but your spirit put me at ease…the book cover is the *first* thing the readers focus their eyes on and you made it so pleasing *and* easy on the eyes–it is exquisite! **Arthur Johnson** and **Kemo Smith,** I'm looking forward to seeing your names on a cover with mine in the *very* near future–we dared to dream, time to cross it off …accomplished!

Thank you, *everyone* for your support! Without you, *the reader*–no purpose would be fulfilled. Thank you so much for being obedient to the Spirit. Beautiful ones…I pray that you are continuously blessed.

And last, but not least.... The plan God has for our future far exceeds any plan we may have envisioned for ourselves, your partnership **Dwayne McLendon** has made my dream a *reality....* Thank you for being obedient to the Holy Spirit; **Dare I Express It – Volume I** is now a seed in which a field of poems *can* and will *grow*.

Dare I Express It

For more books and
about the authors Visit:

www.LeandreaRivers.com
(Leandrea Rivers)

Facebook: D Mack
(Dwayne McLendon)

Dare I Express It

www.ingramcontent.com/pod-product-compliance
Lightning Source LLC
Chambersburg PA
CBHW071456070426
42452CB00040B/1547